Money Clips

THE LITTLE BOOK OF BIG MONEY IDEAS

Money Clips

MICHAEL MATTHEWS

MULTNOMAH BOOKS · SISTERS, OREGON

MONEY CLIPS
© 1994 by Michael D. Matthews
published by Multnomah Books
a part of the Questar Publishing Family
Printed in the United States of America.
International Standard Book Number 0-88070-687-2

All rights reserved.

For information: Questar Publishers, Inc.
Post Office Box 1720, Sisters, Oregon 97759

Unless otherwise indicated, all Scripture references are from the Holy Bible: New International Version, ©
1973, 1978, 1984 by International Bible Society. Used by permission of Zondervan Publishing House. All
rights reserved. The "NIV" and "New International Version" trademarks are registered in the United States
Patent and Trademark Office by International Bible Society. Use of either trademark requires the permission of International Bible Society.

94 95 96 97 98 99 00 01 02 — 10 9 8 7 6 5 4 3 2 1

Matthews, Michael D.
  Money clips: the little book of big money ideas/Michael D. Matthews.
      p. cm
  ISBN 0-88070-687-2: $5.99
  1. Finance, Personal.   2. Saving and investment.   I. Title.
HG179.M3497 1994
332.024–dc20

94-15351
CIP

Dear Reader:

Over the years, I've found that my clients are all hard workers, yet some manage to live very comfortably—no matter what their income—while others are constantly struggling to pay their bills. The difference is in how they plan and handle the money they earn.

My hope for this little book is that it will warn people of some pitfalls and help them plan for the future, so they can relax and enjoy the good life God has given them.

-Mike Matthews, CPA

1.

Pay off your home mortgage
as quickly as you can. Every extra dollar you pay on
principal is the equivalent of
an investment made at a rate of return
equal to the mortgage interest rate.
But first things first…work on reducing high-interest
consumer debt prior to making
substantial principal payments
on your mortgage.

MICHAEL MATTHEWS

2.

Your home will be
the best investment you will ever make,
if you pay off the mortgage early.

3.

Part (or all) of the equity
in your home can turn out to be totally free of
income tax when you eventually sell it.
Up to $125,000 of the increase in the value
of your home can be excluded from income taxation
after you reach age fifty-five,
if certain requirements are met. This is a tremendous
tax-free savings vehicle for you.

4.

Never mortgage your home
to pay off consumer debt unless you lock away
your credit cards and adhere to a time table
for repaying the equity loan.

5.

Make one extra house payment in December
of each year on a thirty-year 7 percent loan and you
will reduce the length of the loan to twenty-four years.

6.

Make extra house payments in June and December
of each year and you will reduce
the length of the loan to about twenty years.

7.

Make extra house payments
in March, June, September, and December
of each year and you will reduce the length of the loan
to fifteen and a half years.

MICHAEL MATTHEWS

8.

Never purchase a home in the mountains
or at the beach as an "investment."
Enjoyment and family fun, however, can't be measured.

9.

A personal budget is a must
for gaining control of your personal finances.

10.

You won't be able to keep track of
how much you are spending with a credit card
unless you have the discipline of a monk.
Use it only for purchases you could pay cash
or write a check for.

11.

Never buy a big-ticket item with a credit card.
Finance it with your bank or credit union.
The lender will make you qualify for the purchase.
If you use a credit card, you may not be honest with
yourself about your ability to repay.

M O N E Y   C L I P S

12.

Avoid purchasing goods
on credit offered by department stores.
Their credit cards have some of the highest
interest rates of all cards.
And "deferred billing plans" of department stores
will often add interest retroactively to the balance.

MICHAEL MATTHEWS

13.

Don't hire a "back slapping" or "glad handing"
accountant or lawyer.

14.

Hire a lawyer to write a will for you and your spouse.
If you don't already know a good lawyer,
interview the five lawyers with the smallest ads
in the Yellow Pages, or ask the Better Business Bureau
for names of lawyers who are members of the BBB.
Ditto for a CPA.

15.

A living trust can be a great tool
for keeping your assets out of the probate process
at the time of your death.
But a living trust won't do any good
unless you transfer your assets into it!

16.

Don't ask a banker for a referral of a lawyer.

MICHAEL MATTHEWS

17.

If your neighbor is a doctor, lawyer, accountant,
insurance agent, Realtor, or stock broker,
don't hire him or her.
It's difficult to fire a neighbor.

18.

Try to buy a car without taking out a loan.
If you must finance your new car, pay the loan off early.

19.

Before putting off saving for college
consider this: Tuition costs are rising
at the rate of 6 to 9 percent each year, far in excess
of the recent rate of inflation.

MICHAEL MATTHEWS

20.

Buy a personal computer. Teach yourself
how to type if you were a jock in high school and
thought typing class was for wimps.
There are some fun, user-friendly
software packages out there that can get your fingers
clicking in no time.

MONEY CLIPS

21.

Learn how to use your computer.
Buy a "bundle" of software and learn how
to use everything in it.

22.

Buy one of the very reasonable home accounting
software packages and use it.
Discuss the results with your spouse. Be honest
with yourself about your debts.

MICHAEL MATTHEWS

23.

Men, your wives will always have better
investment advice than your stock brokers.
Listen to your wife *before* you invest, not after.

24.

Buy disability insurance.
Your chances of benefiting from disability insurance
are greater than your chances of benefiting from
life insurance—although you should own life insurance
at some point in your life.

25.

If you live long enough, you will probably die
without life insurance.
But don't worry—no one
has been left above ground yet.

26.

Don't pay your child to mow your lawn.
He or she has earned the right to do it for free.

MICHAEL MATTHEWS

27.

Never "loan" money to a friend or relative.
Give them the money and ask them to pay it back
if and when they can.
If you consider it a gift in the first place, you won't feel
so badly when they don't repay you.

28.

Cars are a lousy investment. Keep
your cars until they become embarrassing to drive,
unless they fall apart first.

MICHAEL MATTHEWS

29.

After you purchase a new car,
get the repair and maintenance work out of the hands
of the dealer as soon as the warranty permits.
Find a reliable independent mechanic
and stick with him. I lost confidence
in my local dealership when the service technician
fell asleep in the passenger seat while I was driving him
around trying to get the car
to duplicate a mechanical problem.

30.

If leasing a car is for you,
a good deal can be had if you know
the interrelationship between the following:

1. Hard bargaining
2. The dealer's cost
3. Down payment

4. Residual value
5. Length of the lease
6. Monthly payment

31.

Don't let a car sales person know
you are interested in leasing until you have negotiated
your best price for the vehicle you are interested in.
If you bring up leasing before
you know the price of the car, the sales person
will only want to talk about your monthly payment.
Don't get sucked into this trap!

MONEY CLIPS

32.

Remember, leasing a vehicle is a *financing* arrangement.
You are financing the depreciation of the car
during the term of the lease.
The price of the car and the residual you negotiate
are critical to a lease you'll be happy with.

33.

Always shop car insurance.
Never buy insurance from a company
solely because your parents did.

MICHAEL MATTHEWS

34.

Purchase an umbrella insurance policy
to cover yourself against lawsuits in excess of
other policy coverage limits.
Check with the carrier of your homeowner's policy
for this coverage.

35.
Join a membership warehouse
and shop there regularly.
But never go inside without a list,
or you'll find yourself with a new canoe that won't fit
on the top of your car.

36.
Avoid leaving the Home Shopping Network
on your television screen longer than 2.5 seconds.

MICHAEL MATTHEWS

37.
Never use a credit card that charges an annual fee.

38.
Don't buy anything on your credit card
that you can't pay off in full the next month.

39.

Take pride in the fact
that your last credit card statements for the year
show *no interest paid* for the year.

40.

Try to accumulate six months' living expenses
in a savings or money market account.
Just try it! It can't be done!

41.

Use a discount broker.
Employ a full-service broker only if you know how
to spell "ouch."

42.

If your accountant, lawyer, or broker
sends you a newsletter, read every word. You may
have to wade through the sales hype, but you will
always learn something.

M O N E Y   C L I P S

43.

Don't trust the management of your money
to others based upon claims
of an outrageous rate of return.
You will eventually achieve the rate of return
you deserve.

44.

Subscribe to the *Wall Street Journal*
and read it every day. Don't skip the editorial pages,
and don't peek at your mutual funds
ahead of the schedule you've set for yourself.
You'll drive yourself nuts.

45.

You will probably be unhappy with the results
if you lease a car instead of purchasing one.
Yes, the payment is usually lower than purchasing,
but most folks don't have the financial discipline
to *use the difference* to reduce consumer debt or
invest in an interest-bearing account
over the term of the lease.

MICHAEL MATTHEWS

46.
Actuaries are people
who found the study of accounting
to be too exciting.

47.

Your accountant may send you a workbook
to assist you in gathering information
for the preparation of your tax return.
It's a useful tool for both of you.
You are less likely to overlook pertinent information,
and your accountant can prepare
your return in less time, resulting in a lower fee.

M I C H A E L   M A T T H E W S

48.

Car insurance rates may be lower in the town
where your son or daughter attends college.
Ask your insurance agent if you can save some money
by changing the address on your child's auto policy
to the college town during the school year.

49.

Consider using a professional negotiator
for the purchaser of your next new car.
You will probably end up with a much better deal
than trying to negotiate the sale on your own.
Most of us are easy pickings for car sales people.

MICHAEL MATTHEWS

50.

If tax shelters come back into fashion,
run from any promoter who approaches you.
He or she will be easy to spot. They were selling
batteries last week at the local Radio Shack.

51.

Enter the Publisher's Clearing House drawing
every year.
Somebody really does win the thing.

MONEY CLIPS

52.

Don't build a new house
unless your marriage is stronger
than that of any couple you know.

53.

Start a savings account when your child is
twelve years old for future car expenses.
You'll need it when your son or daughter
smashes your car into a guard rail
in the middle of the night.
It'll be cheaper to pay for the damages yourself
than to suffer through at least three years
of increased insurance premiums.

M O N E Y   C L I P S

54.

Young drivers in your household
are a second good reason to keep your cars
until they embarrass you.

55.

Get to know the owner of an auto body shop that
charges less than others in town.
They won't be hard to find. Just ask a friend or
business associate who has kids
about eighteen months older than yours.

MICHAEL MATTHEWS

56.

If you have to hide money in that secret compartment
of your wallet to protect you from yourself,
try paying a little extra on the principal
of your mortgage.
Make a solemn oath with yourself not to borrow
against the equity in your home—ever.

57.

Don't take up golf for business purposes.
Business has enough inherent frustrations
without intentionally adding others.

58.

Don't join a country club for business purposes.
Most everyone else who belongs to the club
is there to pick up business if they can.
And the club dues are no longer deductible.

MICHAEL MATTHEWS

59.

Swallow your pride and consult with
a consumer credit counseling agency in your area
if you are in financial trouble.
They will help you identify your debts and contact your
creditors to arrange a payment schedule.

60.

Throw away every unsolicited credit card application
you receive in the mail.

61.

When your child leaves for college,
apply for a credit card in his or her name
only if you are reasonably certain your child is
financially responsible.
You will have to co-sign for the card,
but you will be helping your son or daughter
establish a credit history.

M I C H A E L   M A T T H E W S

62.

One thing is as certain as death and taxes…college costs *will* rise at a rate higher than the rate of inflation. You must start saving for your children's college educations when they are infants if you want both you and them to be free of debt when they graduate. Start college savings accounts for your kids in mutual funds geared toward growth, and have a plan for determining when to switch the focus of the investments as college age nears.

63.
Don't buy a hot tub.
Dad told me we wouldn't use it for very long.
He was right.

64.
Listen to your elders.
Those older than us have probably made all
the financial mistakes we are about to make. Maybe
we can allow them to save us from ourselves.

M I C H A E L   M A T T H E W S

65.

Make your kids work a couple of crummy jobs
before they graduate from high school.
Try and arrange for them to work in a place
where they will have a jerk for a boss.

66.

If you're a Denver Bronco or Buffalo Bills fan,
never go to a Super Bowl to watch them play,
even if you have relatives in the host city
and you can save the cost of a hotel room.
The humiliation just isn't worth it.

MICHAEL MATTHEWS

67.

Real estate investing can be heart-breaking,
and the equivalent of a glacier for your money.
Either get in and out quickly,
or try to pay it off and hold it until you die.

68.

Consider purchasing long-term care insurance
for your parents. You and your siblings
could team up to purchase insurance to offset the cost
of nursing home care you may incur
if your parents do not have the funds.
The timing of this insurance purchase is critical.
You should carefully research the various policy
features available. Long-term care insurance
is becoming a hot insurance contact.

M I C H A E L   M A T T H E W S

69.

Don't buy a motor home unless you plan to be on the
road at least THREE MONTHS out of the year.
Otherwise, you could stay in a five-star hotel
for what the motor home will cost you.

70.

Everyone should have a will. Don't allow the state
to determine the disposition of your assets,
and don't allow your family to descend into
a protracted squabble over your estate.

71.

Success in one's chosen business, trade, or profession
does not translate into success in investing
simply by osmosis.
Do what you do best and be very careful about the rest.

72.

Points paid on the purchase of a new home
are generally deductible.
Points paid on a refinancing are deductible
over the term of the loan.

MICHAEL MATTHEWS

73.

Points from a prior refinance of your home mortgage
not yet deducted become fully deductible
in the year the mortgage is refinanced.

74.

Buy a new car no more than twice during your life.
Purchase used cars and let someone else
take the hit for the severe decrease in value
over the first year or two
of the life of the car.

MONEY CLIPS

75.
Do not covet thy neighbor's car.

76.
Courtesy counts in business,
as in all other aspects in life.
Say thank you to customers, clients,
and those who refer business to you.

MICHAEL MATTHEWS

77.

Partnerships should not be entered into lightly.
Go in with both eyes open
and both hands on your wallet.

78.

Never enter into a partnership or corporate ownership
with others without a partnership agreement
or a buy-sell agreement.

79.

You never truly know another individual until you marry that person or make him or her your partner or fellow shareholder in business.

80.

Before you start your own business,
reflect soberly on the fact that the vast majority
of small businesses fail within the first five years.

81.

You can't turn yourself into a car by living in a garage.
Not everyone has the skill and temperament
to own a business.

82.

Don't start a business with the expectation of
providing a job for your children
or other family members. It could turn out to be
the biggest mistake of your life.

83.

If you want to start a retirement plan for
your small business, other than an IRA,
do not use a prototype plan from a stock broker.
Nine times out of ten, your broker will not know
enough about retirement plans to keep your plan
document updated to qualify with the IRS.

MICHAEL MATTHEWS

84.

A business retirement plan with the slightest amount of
complexity should be administered by
a retirement plan specialist.

85.

You will never own the most advanced
personal computer on the market.
It will always be on the dealer's shelf.

86.
Clipping coupons (and using them)
should become a habit.

87.
Christmas or Hanukkah shopping habits
are the weakest link in most people's spending patterns.
A budget is critical to gaining control
of your holiday purchases.

MICHAEL MATTHEWS

88.

There are no quick fixes
for a poor credit history.
Only the passage of time can remove a trail
of unfavorable reports
from your credit record.

89.

Credit bureaus collect information
about all of us that is reported to them
by credit card companies, banks, department stores,
and others. Accurate negative credit information is
retained in your credit history for seven years.
Bankruptcy information is retained for ten years.

M I C H A E L   M A T T H E W S

90.

Mark this: You can correct incorrect or
outdated information in your credit report.
You have the right to receive
a copy of your credit history.
Unless you have been denied credit within
the last thirty days, you will have to pay a fee
of $5 to $20 for a copy of your credit report.

91.

The credit bureau is required by law
to explain your credit history to you. Obtain a copy
of your credit report and ask about any entries
you do not fully understand.

92.

Discuss any incorrect or outdated information in
your credit history with the credit bureau.
The bureau must investigate any information
you disagree with—at no charge to you.

MICHAEL MATTHEWS

93.

If the credit bureau discovers
the items in your credit report that you disagree with
are incorrect, the bureau must send a corrected copy
of your report to anyone who received
the incorrect information within the past 180 days.

94.

You have the right to include a statement of up to
one hundred words in your credit history
explaining why you disagree with an entry in your file.
This explanation will be included
in your credit report.

95.

Accurate data in your credit history cannot be removed
by companies advertising "credit repair" services.
Be wary of advertisements promising to fix bad credit.

MICHAEL MATTHEWS

96.

If you are having trouble paying your bills,
contact the companies you owe money to
and try to work out a payment arrangement.
Don't ignore billing and collection notices.
Most creditors are willing to work out
extended payment arrangements.

97.

The tax rules regarding sales and replacements
of personal residences are complex.
Don't shoot yourself in the foot
by entering into a transaction without consulting
an accountant or attorney.

MICHAEL MATTHEWS

98.

After you purchase your first home,
start a file for improvements you make to the home.
Every receipt counts, but you need to know
the difference between an improvement
and a repair.

99.

When you sell your home and purchase a new one,
always place a copy of Form 2119 from your
income tax return in your home improvements file.
Then you won't have to search for a copy of the return
containing this form ten or twenty years from now.

100.

A loss on the sale of your personal residence
is not deductible.

101.

If you are planning to build your dream home,
don't buy the land more than two years
before you can build and occupy the place.
You could find yourself
with unexpected income tax to pay.

102.

A five-word sure-fire way to make a small fortune
in all of the following investments:

—Commodities   —Precious metals
—Horse breeding   —Options trading
—The restaurant business   —Section 8 housing
                    —Diamonds

START WITH A LARGE FORTUNE!

MICHAEL MATTHEWS

103.

When buying life insurance, stay away from
"whole life" policies. Buy "term" insurance
and a good mutual fund instead. Consider "whole life"
only if you must force yourself to save—
and can't do it in any other way.

104.

Never buy a stock after reading a favorable story
in the *Wall Street Journal*.
The entire world already knows about it.

105.

If your son or daughter becomes a stock broker,
wish him well, cheer her on, but hire
someone else as your broker.

106.

Don't talk yourself into an investment
with all borrowed money. You probably won't make
any money if you don't have anything invested.

MICHAEL MATTHEWS

107.

The Securities and Exchange Commission requires
all public companies to file Form 10-K.
It is one of the best sources
of information available about a company.
Part of your research of a stock should include
Form 10-K. Anyone can obtain a copy of this form
by contacting the investor relations department of
the target company.

108.

When you have a child, start two mutual funds:
one for orthodontics and the other for college.

109.

Never underestimate the erosive power of inflation.
It will eat away your income and savings
at the same time.

M I C H A E L   M A T T H E W S

110.

The other side of the coin: If you own real estate,
inflation can be good for you.

111.

The financial side of your marriage
should be like a successful partnership.
All investments and other decisions involving money
should be discussed and carefully considered
together with your spouse.

MONEY CLIPS

112.

The best investments are probably
right under your nose.
Take a look at where you and your kids spend money.
You might find the next Wal-Mart
right in your backyard.

113.

If you are interested in investing in individual stocks,
join the National Association of Investors Corporation.
The NAIC provides training tools for investment
analysis, investment club data, and access to stock
dividend reinvestment programs, among other things.

114.

Get to know a couple of DRIPs
(dividend reinvestment programs).
You may even be able to purchase stocks at a discount.

115.

Don't fool yourself into believing
you can "time" the stock market.
Guessing when a stock or mutual fund is at its highest
or lowest price is next to impossible.
Invest for the long term. Buy and sell on
the fundamentals, not on hunches.

M I C H A E L   M A T T H E W S

116.

Don't assume that all tax-exempt municipal bonds
are safe investments.
Thoroughly explore the risk and volatility
of these securities before investing.

117.

Use a fee-only financial planner instead
of a financial planner who also sells products.
The fees you pay a fee-only planner are stated
in black and white, not hidden in the commission
in financial products sold by the planner. A fee-only
planner will recommend products that are entirely
in your best interest.

MICHAEL MATTHEWS

118.

Husbands have a tendency to make all of the financial
and investment decisions for the family.
If the wife defers to the husband in these matters,
she must become familiar with the family finances
in the event her husband dies first.

119.

Small investors:
Beware of spending a small fortune
on investment publications, newsletters,
and mutual fund rating services.

120.

Visit your public library and ask
about the financial, income tax, and investment
resource material available there.
Many of the most commonly used publications
for investment research are at your library.
Save your money and get a library card.

121.

Check with your broker about the research materials
available at his or her office.

122.

Your tolerance for risk
will dictate your style of investing.
You may be very conservative, because—it's true—
you can't fall off the floor.
But remember, inflation is your worst enemy
if you are saving and investing
for college costs and retirement.

123.

The best protection your investments will have
against inflation is the stock market.
Some portion of what you have should be
in the market at all times, in the form of
stocks or mutual funds.
You will have to determine the mix that is best for you.
Even if you use the services of a full-service broker,
you must educate yourself about the history
and workings of the stock market.

MICHAEL MATTHEWS

124.

Investing in the stock market is important because
stocks and mutual funds may pay you income
in the form of dividends. But they also afford you
the opportunity to make your money grow
through increases in the value of the stocks
and mutual funds shares as the economy expands.
That is your hedge against the eroding
power of inflation. Certificates of deposit will pay
interest to you, but they will not appreciate in value.

125.

To become comfortable with some degree of risk,
you must understand how the various types
of investments work.
Subscribe to a personal finance magazine,
and read several books about investing and
financial planning. Relying solely on the advice of
others (brokers, neighbors, accountants, insurance sales
people, your brother-in-law) could be hazardous
to your financial health.

MICHAEL MATTHEWS

126.

Your tolerance for risk can realistically be measured
only after you have gained some insight
into the workings of the financial markets.
Old prejudices against the stock market drilled into you
by your parents or others may have implanted
unjustified fears into your thinking.
Such fears could prevent you from reaping
financial rewards. Aim for a sensible,
balanced approach to risk.

127.

No matter how much you learn about investments,
your fear of risk may still cause you to lose sleep
and suffer undue stress.
It isn't worth it. If your investments
are keeping you awake at night, by all means
reduce the risk in your portfolio.
No matter what others tell you,
they don't have to live with your fears.

MICHAEL MATTHEWS

128.

Diversify your investments.
Everybody knows that, right?
But many people still don't do it.
That hot tip from your brother-in-law, or the hunch
you have from reading *The Wall Street Journal*,
will cause you to become over-concentrated
in one stock or mutual fund.

129.

Stocks and mutual funds can be
unbeatable investments. But don't invest everything
you have in the stock market.
You must have enough funds in liquid investments—
such as savings and money market accounts—
to see you through short-term cash needs
and unexpected emergencies.
Here's a rule of thumb: Subtract your age from
one hundred. The result is the percentage of your capital
that should be invested in stocks and mutual funds.

MICHAEL MATTHEWS

130.

Try to teach your children about the magic of compounding. You might be surprised at how interested children can become in saving and investing when you show them how quickly money can accumulate.

131.

The "Rule of 72" is useful for determining
how long it will take to double any investment.
Simply divide the rate of return from an investment
into seventy-two, and you will have the approximate
period of time over which your investment will double.
But don't forget about taxes in your equation!
Either reduce the rate of return by the tax effect,
or plan to pay the taxes
from some other source of cash.

MICHAEL MATTHEWS

132.

Net asset value (NAV) is the market value of
one mutual fund share.

133.

Don't sell small amounts
of a mutual fund if you can avoid doing so.
You'll drive your accountant nuts trying to keep track
of your basis from year to year.
If you need cash periodically
and have no other source but your mutual fund,
take dividends from the fund in cash
rather than reinvesting them.

MICHAEL MATTHEWS

134.
Don't always avoid mutual funds
that charge a sales load.

135.
Buy a couple of mutual funds
and invest in them regularly.
Stay away from the Singapore Pork Belly Fund
and the European Coffee Futures Fund.

136.

After you buy your mutual funds, steel yourself
against following them every day in the paper.
Look at the price about once a month.
And never decide to sell them on Sunday morning.

MICHAEL MATTHEWS

137.

The preferable method of investing in mutual funds
is to purchase shares in the fund
over a long period of time.
This method is called "dollar cost averaging."

138.

Invest in a mutual fund every month
after your initial investment.
Authorize your bank to accept a draft on your account
from the fund in an amount you have pre-authorized.
This method ensures that you will not invent an excuse
to avoid your monthly investment in the fund.
You will find yourself creating reasons not to invest in
the mutual fund about every other month if you choose
to invest in the fund by writing a check each month
instead of using a draft.

MICHAEL MATTHEWS

139.

Start an Individual Retirement Account
the first time you find yourself on someone's payroll.
Keep funding your IRA until you retire
(or until you reach age seventy and a half).
Also, keep every tax return you file after
you become eligible for your employer's retirement plan.
You'll need them to keep track of your basis.

140.

Never purchase tax-exempt municipal bonds
in your retirement plan or IRA account.

141.

Social security is not intended
to replace your income after you retire.
It should be a small part
of your retirement planning.

142.

Being eligible for full benefits under social security
entitles you to receive a benefit.
The amount of your benefit, however,
depends upon your lifetime earnings.
The higher your cumulative earnings,
the greater your benefit.

MICHAEL MATTHEWS

143.

Surprise! You may not be eligible for full social security
benefits when you reach age sixty-five.
Look up your year of birth in the following table to
determine your eligible retirement age:

Year Born	Retirement Age
• 1960 and later	67
• 1959	66 and 10 months
• 1958	66 and 8 months
• 1957	66 and 6 months
• 1956	66 and 4 months
• 1955	66 and 2 months
• 1943-1954	66
• 1942	65 and 10 months
• 1941	65 and 8 months
• 1940	65 and 6 months
• 1939	65 and 4 months
• 1938	65 and 2 months
• 1937 and earlier	65

MICHAEL MATTHEWS

144.

If you delay your retirement beyond
normal retirement age, you will receive an increased
social security benefit, depending upon how many
additional years you work.

145.

If you receive social security benefits
and continue to work, your benefits will be reduced
if your earnings exceed certain amounts.
After age seventy, however, there is no income limit.

MICHAEL MATTHEWS

146.

Supplemental Security Income (SSI) pays monthly benefits to those with low incomes and limited assets who are sixty-five or older, blind, or disabled. Children under age eighteen can also qualify. Check with your local social security office regarding these rules.

147.
Never represent yourself in an IRS audit
if you did not prepare your own income tax return.

148.

Claim the family pet as a dependent on
your tax return only if you are able to obtain
a social security number for it!

149.

If you give away more than 5 percent
of your gross income, always attach copies
of your canceled checks and receipts
for charitable contributions
to your income tax return.

MICHAEL MATTHEWS

150.

Hire a CPA or other tax professional
to prepare your income tax return.
Don't do your own tax return if you own a house.

151.

If your tax return contains even a modest degree of
complexity, do it yourself only with the aid of a
quality tax preparation computer program.

MICHAEL MATTHEWS

152.

Don't hesitate to extend
your income tax return filing date
if you need more time.
The IRS will not target your return for audit
solely because you filed for an extension.

153.

If you must go to the IRS office for an audit
of your tax return, never lose your temper
with the IRS agent or office auditor,
no matter how they may rake you over the coals.
You can ask for a conference with the agent's
supervisor if you believe you are being mistreated,
but ask for the meeting after the agent
has finished his or her report.

MICHAEL MATTHEWS

154.

During an IRS audit, try to make the agent stick only to the issues in the audit letter by emphasizing that you (or the representative there with you) prepared for the audit based upon the issues identified in the letter.

155.

Don't volunteer information during an audit by the IRS. Answer only the questions you are asked.

156.

Try to control the order of the information you give to an IRS agent during an audit. Give the agent data that answer questions completely before you get to the issues that you know may be adjusted.

If, for instance, you can establish credibility with very complete records for charitable contributions and follow that up with well documented receipts for business meals and entertainment, the IRS auditor may be more receptive to your "reconstruction" of business auto mileage than if you presented mileage information first.

MICHAEL MATTHEWS

157.

Don't rely solely on the answers the IRS gives you
over its toll-free information line.
They are wrong enough of the time to cause you
problems. You have no defense if you rely
on incorrect information the IRS gives
over the telephone.

158.

Don't hesitate to file an amended income tax return
if something you put on a return
is keeping you awake at night.
Yes, you may have to write a check,
but...there's nothing like a good night's sleep.

159.

Never create tax deductions just for the sake of
saving taxes. This includes interest deductions.
Creating deductions will work only if
the marginal tax rate reaches 100 percent or higher.
(Stay tuned for that one.)

160.

Itemized deductions can be "bunched" into alternate
years to take full advantage of both
your itemized deductions and the standard deduction.
But if it's a close call, watch out
for the *time value* of money.

M I C H A E L   M A T T H E W S

161.

Never give to a charity over the telephone, particularly charities that have the words "Police Protective" in their names.

162.

If you are in doubt about the tax status of a charity, check it out by visiting your local IRS office and asking for Publication 78, *Cumulative List of Organizations*.

163.

Don't hesitate to ask a charity for its most recent
financial statements if you want to know
how it is spending money.
Ask questions about the percentage of its expenses
that is going for fund raising. If the answers you receive
are vague or evasive, it's time to direct
your generosity elsewhere.

MICHAEL MATTHEWS

164.

Remember: Canceled checks are no longer
good enough proof for the IRS
of charitable contributions of $250 or more.
You must obtain a receipt from the charity.

165.

If you are a teacher or work for a not-for-profit entity,
put as much as you can stand into
a tax-sheltered annuity.
Pay particular attention to the "catch up" provision
available to you if you've been employed there
but haven't previously used
this retirement vehicle.

166.

Have some sympathy for your accountant
toward the middle of April.
If you owe him or her a couple of pieces of information
to finish up your tax return, don't wait until April 10th
and then expect your return by the 15th.
At the very least, bring the missing information
to your accountant's office on April 10th
inside a box of donuts.

M O N E Y   C L I P S

167.

Keep a careful, complete mileage log
if you use your car for business. You haven't squirmed
in a long time like you will when you face
the IRS auditor and try to justify how you came up
with 99.5 percent "business use" of your car when
your average daily commute is twenty miles.
The auditor will quickly do the math and inform you
that your total miles had to have been
one million for that year. End of discussion.

MICHAEL MATTHEWS

168.

Yes, taxes *are* too high
and the government *does* waste much of what we pay.
But that's no license to cheat on your taxes.
What tax cheats don't pay is made up by the rest of us;
the government doesn't seem to reduce its expenditures
by what tax cheats don't contribute.

M O N E Y   C L I P S

169.

If you move, your employer might reimburse you for
moving expenses far in excess of those you can deduct.
Be sure your withholding tax is sufficient to cover
the additional tax, or save an equivalent amount
to avoid an April shock.
And watch out for the penalty
for underpayment of estimated tax.

MICHAEL MATTHEWS

170.

Stamps, coins, and precious metals held for investment
are capital assets. Any gain or loss
from their sale is capital gain or loss,
unless you are a dealer in such items.

171.

If you are a small business owner, don't even *think* about not paying your payroll tax deposits in a timely manner. The IRS deals harshly with those who try to make use of payroll tax funds for working capital. Payroll tax disasters can result because tax deposits not made can amount to very large sums over a short period of time. Penalties and interest on top of the tax can be the undoing of the business in the hands of an aggressive collections official.

MICHAEL MATTHEWS

172.

Do not allow your social security number or that of your spouse to be used to report interest and dividend income on accounts that belong to your children.

173.

Find that delicate balance that allows you to reduce debt, save, invest, and plan for a long life…
but live each day as if it were your last.

174.

Take a vacation every year.
In fact, take *several* if you can swing it.

MICHAEL MATTHEWS

175.

Go to Hawaii at least once before you die,
preferably before you start using a walker.
And take a half-day snorkeling boat to Molokini
if you ever get to Maui.

176.

The crushing weight of debt
will intensify anyone's mid-life crisis.
The more debt you have,
the earlier middle age arrives.

MICHAEL MATTHEWS

177.

Seeking satisfaction from possessions and wealth
will blind you from recognizing
what is truly sufficient.

178.

Sufficiency will be yours
when you can start measuring what you have
against what others lack,
rather than longing for what others have.

M I C H A E L   M A T T H E W S

179.

Debt can quickly become the rudder
that steers your life.
A potentially oppressive force,
it can enslave you and cut you off
from your treasured pursuits.

180.

Before you can begin to pull yourself out of
the debt trap, sit down and make a complete list of
your debts. You might be surprised to find
how far you've descended into the hole. Then again,
you might discover that "digging out"—even if
painful—will actually be do-able.

MICHAEL MATTHEWS

181.

Selling assets is a source of cash for getting out of debt.
Before you do that, however, carefully
calculate income taxes due on such sales.
Don't overlook the alternative minimum tax.

182.

Regular charitable giving can break the hold
money has on your life.

183.

Measure what you keep, not what you earn.

184.

Never measure *yourself* by what you keep
or by what you earn.

185.

Learn the difference between saving and hoarding.

MONEY CLIPS

186.

Don't save 5 percent and give away 5 percent.
Save until it hurts, and give away
as much as you can.

187.

Don't adjust your expenditures to match your income.

188.

Offer a little "sweat equity" to your church
or a charity or two in your community.
You have a skill that is valuable to some volunteer
organization in need of help. Your time can be as useful
and encouraging to them as your money.
And it will do something for you, too.

MICHAEL MATTHEWS

189.

Approach financial problems *with* your spouse.
Don't try to solve such problems alone,
or shoulder the blame for a financial mess
you probably have created together.

190.

Walk away from get-rich-quick schemes.
One mistake can cause years of financial agony,
along with a severe strain on your marriage.

191.

Take the "tortoise" approach to your personal
finances. A long-term view of wealth accumulation
is the historically proven attitude
that you must develop.

192.

Talk to your children periodically
about the proper role of money in their lives.
Don't lecture them about it.
Seek opportunities to point out truths you want them
to learn as
real-life situations present themselves.

193.

"Godliness with contentment is great gain.
For we brought nothing into the world,
and we can take nothing out of it.
But if we have food and clothing, we will be content
with that" (1 Timothy 6:6-8).

MONEY CLIPS

194.

"People who want to get rich fall into temptation
and a trap and into many foolish and harmful desires
that plunge men into ruin and destruction.
For the love of money is a root of all kinds of evil.
Some people, eager for money, have wandered
from the faith and pierced themselves
with many griefs" (1 Timothy 6:9-10).

MICHAEL MATTHEWS